ELIZABETH DREW

FEAR

AND LOATHING IN GEORGE W. BUSH'S WASHINGTON

PREFACE BY RUSSELL BAKER

as published in The New York Review of Books

NEW YORK REVIEW BOOKS, NEW YORK

THIS IS A NEW YORK REVIEW BOOK

PUBLISHED BY THE NEW YORK REVIEW OF BOOKS

FEAR AND LOATHING IN GEORGE W. BUSH'S WASHINGTON
by Elizabeth Drew

This edition published in 2004 in the United States of America by
The New York Review of Books, 1755 Broadway, New York, NY 10019
www.nyrb.com

Book and cover design by Milton Glaser, Inc.

Library of Congress Cataloging-in-Publication Data
Drew, Elizabeth.
Fear and loathing in George W. Bush's America / Elizabeth Drew ;
preface by Russell Baker.
p. cm.
ISBN 1-59017-128-4 (pbk. : alk. paper)
1. United States—Politics and government—2001- 2. Bush, George W. (George Walker),
1946- 3. Rove, Karl. 4. Political culture—United States. 5. Fear—Political aspects—
United States. 6. Aversion—Political aspects—United States. 7. Political parties—United
States. 8. Conservatism—United States. I. Title.
E902.D74 2004
306.2'0973'090511—dc22
                                          2004010694
ISBN 1-59017-128-4

Printed in the United States of America on acid-free paper.

June 2004

1 3 5 7 9 10 8 6 4 2

CONTENTS

PREFACE

IN WASHINGTON AN AGE OF MORAL AND PHILOSOPHICAL STERILITY is deeply entrenched, and as Elizabeth Drew's reporting attests, the result is not pretty. The decline dates from the end of the cold war, which suddenly and shockingly left Washington without any purpose that could be called visionary or even faintly noble.

Since then government has seemed to be mostly about raising money to get elected, and then reelected repeatedly in order to service those who put up the money. There is no moral urgency in it, no philosophical imperative at work.

Not surprisingly, accounts of Washington doings are suffused with a sense of pointlessness, a suspicion that it is an insider's game not meant for rubes. Even the rancorous abuse that passes for political discourse feels phony—billingsgate designed to manipulate a dulled electorate. Manipulation is now such a common way of life that Washington has invented a word for it—"spinning"—and the press reports admiringly on how the press itself is "spun" by cunning "spinmeisters."

In this atmosphere history has a dreamlike quality. A war is said to be in progress, and the President describes himself as "a war president," but, except for military professionals, no one is asked to fight or sacrifice or even, as in World War II, to save waste fats and grease. We are asked only to shop with a generous hand, to accept a tax cut, and to be scared.

Being scared when war is in progress is no longer considered cowardly. In olden days Americans did not scare, no matter how grave the danger. Beset by truly formidable foes in the 1940s, they exulted with foolish and utterly unjustified cockiness in their certitude of victory. With Spike Jones they sang, "Heil! Heil! Right in der Führer's face." Unlike today's worried patriots, they were swashbucklers. Citizens eager to become warriors.

Now fear is officially authorized. Fear manipulators issue baffling color-coded "alerts" and hair-raising speeches. As this is written, Vice President Cheney is on television in the next room raising goose bumps on an audience of Republican money donors. He praises the satanic ingenuity of the axis of evil. He hints at possible nuclear catastrophe. Death and devastation are near.

And maybe they are, but between now and then might not Washington think of some attitude more uplifting than a cringe? In Washington a president once made a devastated nation's spirit soar by delivering a pep speech. Nothing to fear, he said, but fear itself.

Speeches that lift the spirit would sound false from the Washington operatives of whom Elizabeth Drew writes. Speechwriters still abound, but now they dream of the perfect manipulative sound bite: "read my lips," "I feel your pain," "axis of evil."

The absence of any purpose more interesting than surviving another election probably explains why the men in Ms. Drew's essays strike us as small-time connivers rather than creative thinkers, or dreamers, or even statesmen. This may be unfair; if so, they must blame the sterility of the age in which they work.

Karl Rove exemplifies the new Washington man: the almost perfect technician, a man dedicated to piloting an affable if unengaged figurehead president through the tricky shoals of governance, and doing it so artfully that reelection must result.

For this work no grasp of Hamiltonian and Jeffersonian theories of governance is needed, or ability to grapple with moral ambiguity, or any of what the first President Bush called "the vision thing." Though Rove may be richly skilled in these departments, it would be professionally unforgivable to apply them in his work.

The chief necessities of his office are an endless supply of polls and a technical skill at interpreting them. Correctly interpreted and acted upon ruthlessly, they will lead his client to another term in the White House.

Rove is not a new political phenomenon. Bill Clinton had a Karl Rove named Dick Morris, a hired gun ready to help elect anyone ready to pay, regardless of party. As Bush trims policy to follow Rove's course to reelected glory, so Clinton trimmed at Morris's direction. In the process Clinton moved away from the old Democratic liberals and ended up slightly to the right of Nelson Rockefeller.

Under Rove's political advice, Bush also seems to be taking

on strange new political coloring. On first taking office he seemed bent on repealing the previous sixty-five years of American history and restoring the economics of the Harding-Coolidge-Hoover regnum. Maybe he even hoped to go back to Mark Hanna: 1896 restored to glory! An end of all taxes on capital and the moneyed classes!

He was quick enough to put Theodore Roosevelt behind him. TR had been unkind to corporations. He had tainted Hanna's economic Darwinism with "progressivism," chatter about the environment, and similar nonsense. Bush, to accommodate the oil, coal, timber, and mining industries, put the boot into environmentalism, granted indulgences to water and air polluters, and decided not to worry about global warming.

But matters have since taken a bizarre turn. Bush is now the father of history's most gigantic budget deficit, which makes him the philosophical heir to Franklin Roosevelt. Generations of conservatives saw the devil in FDR's red ink, and true believers still do.

So did Paul O'Neill, Bush's first secretary of the treasury. When O'Neill fretted about it, Vice President Cheney told him Reagan had proved that deficits don't matter, and fired him.

A lot of the deficit results from Bush's startling decision to force passage of a multibillion-dollar Medicare drug program, although his deep tax cuts for the wealthy had already depleted the treasury. Such programs have been despised and denounced by generations of Republicans as the work of bleeding-heart, big-spending liberalism, but political considerations seemed to be pushing Bush further and further into the New Deal way of life.

The war on terror accounts for another big part of the deficit. After the successful and popular war against Afghanistan's Taliban government came the still baffling decision to invade Iraq and put an American army in the Middle East, if not the most dangerous area on the planet, certainly one bound to drain American wealth for years to come.

Here is another exotic political turn. In the 2000 campaign Bush opposed "nation building." Now he proposes to protect freedom in Iraq until a new democratic nation emerges. Why we are in Iraq at all may not be clear for years to come. There was no cause to suppose that the Iraqi dictator Saddam Hussein was anything but hostile to the al-Qaeda terrorists. Yet the Bush people immediately took the September 11 attacks as an occasion for war on Iraq.

There are various explanations. One has it that the Bush people were determined on it from their first days in office, long before September 11.[1] This would suggest a political motive: Bush's father had been criticized for not taking Baghdad and finishing Saddam in the 1991 war. If the son waded in and did the job right he might gain political points with his party's bellicose elements.

The authors of Bush's Middle East policy, however, seem to have been planning it throughout the Clinton years. They were a small conservative foreign policy clique based in the Pentagon, home office of the military-industrial complex.

This is now such a vast power structure that it is something of a government within the government, and like a separate government it now has its own foreign policy. Secretary of Defense Rumsfeld has often talked as if he were also secretary of state, not hesitating to insult France and Germany for refusing to join the "coalition of the willing."

The Pentagon's foreign policy division not only paved the road to war, but also seem to have inspired the astonishing decision to depart from tradition and commit the United States to a radical new policy of waging unilateral preventive war. The State Department is not much heard from, but it goes along quietly. Like the rest of Washington since the cold war ended so abruptly, it seems to be waiting for an idea to turn up.

—RUSSELL BAKER

FOOTNOTE

1 Two recent books present evidence for this conclusion: Ron Suskind, *The Price of Loyalty: George W. Bush, the White House, and the Education of Paul O'Neill* (Simon and Schuster, 2004), and Richard Clarke, *Against All Enemies: Inside America's War on Terror* (Free Press, 2004).

FEAR

FEAR AND LOATHING
IN GEORGE W. BUSH'S
WASHINGTON

As published in *The New York Review of Books*
May 1, 2003

THE ENFORCER

*Bush's Brain: How Karl Rove Made
George W. Bush Presidential*
by James Moore and Wayne Slater.
Wiley, 395 pp., $27.95

*Boy Genius: Karl Rove, the Brains Behind
the Remarkable Political Triumph of George W. Bush*
by Lou Dubose, Jan Reid, and Carl M. Cannon.
PublicAffairs, 253 pp., $15.00 (paper)

• •

NO PREVIOUS PRESIDENTIAL AIDE HAS HAD THE POWER and influence that Karl Rove has in the White House of George W. Bush. He has been Bush's closest adviser since he first ran for governor of Texas. The authors of *Bush's Brain* write that during Bush's six years as governor of Texas "nothing important happened without his [Rove's] imprimatur." Yet Rove's work takes place behind the scenes; he rarely gives television interviews. Most of his activities are carried out in secrecy, and other White House officials are very reluctant to talk about what he does. The Bush White House is more clamped down than any other in recent history: Bush hates leaks, which he believes damaged his father's reelection chances, and Rove is his enforcer.

Both of the recent biographies of Karl Rove concentrate on his role in Texas politics and in Bush's rise, but they go a long way toward helping us understand Bush's presidency. The more recent one, *Bush's Brain*, by James Moore and Wayne Slater, two experienced Texas reporters who have covered the pair for many years, has fresh information about Rove's influence on Bush. *Boy Genius*, Bush's edgy nickname for Rove, by two Texas reporters as well as Carl Cannon, a writer for the conservative *Weekly Standard*, goes over much of the same

ground but is less probing about Rove's fascinating, and trou-
bling, character, and his relationship with Bush.

Both books tell us about the heretofore-little-explored early
relationship between Bush and Rove and show how it developed. The fifty-two-year-old Rove, a self-described "nerd" who
likes nothing more than studying political history and ana-
lyzing electoral statistics, was born in Colorado in 1950, the son
of a mineral geologist whose family moved about the country.
He spent most of his early years in what he calls a "relatively
conservative state," Utah; he attended the university there and
later the University of Texas, as well as George Mason University, and never took a degree. He has a somewhat profes-
sorial manner (when he's not red-faced and vituperatively on
the attack), and has read widely, especially in American history.

Rove made his first important political connections as an
officer of the national group called College Republicans,
which has branches on hundreds of campuses and has produced a number of well-known political operators on the
right, several of whom Rove has worked with. They include
the late Lee Atwater, who became a model for Rove and
helped to advance his career; the late Terry Dolan, the
founder of the first sophisticated right-wing political organization, the National Conservative Political Action Committee,
or NCPAC; Ralph Reed, the former executive director of the
Christian Coalition and now a flourishing political consult-

ant (he was instrumental in Bush's campaign for the nomination, in particular using his phone banks on behalf of Bush during the South Carolina primary); and Grover Norquist, founder and head of Americans for Tax Reform and the organizer of a coalition of some one hundred groups on the right, all dedicated to reducing the role of government.

In 1973, with Atwater's help, Rove ran successfully for national chairman of the College Republicans. According to a current associate, he remembers to this day exactly who was for him and who opposed him. From Atwater, with whom Rove worked soon after in an election in South Carolina, he got an early introduction to the ways of South Carolina politics. Atwater was a native of the state as well as responsible for much of the distinctive barbarity of its political campaigns. That experience was to prove invaluable in Bush's victory there in 2000. Atwater also taught Rove how to make the most of such "wedge" issues as patriotism and race in order to divide the opposition. Thus, after being badly beaten by John McCain in New Hampshire, Bush made a calculated appearance at South Carolina's Bob Jones University, which banned interracial dating, thus appealing to the fundamentalist vote.

Rove's chairmanship of the College Republicans in the mid-1970s allowed him to frequent the offices of the

Republican National Committee when it was headed by the elder George Bush, who hired him as his personal assistant. (One of Rove's assignments was to turn over the father's keys when his eldest son came to town and wanted to use a family car.) Later, Rove moved to Austin to help the elder Bush's presidential campaign. Rove came to see son George, who was then part-owner of the Texas Rangers baseball team, as having political promise and sensed he might be the ideal instrument for fulfilling Rove's own ambition to have national power. He steadily nudged George W. toward running first for the governorship of Texas, and then for president. The consultant, as the recent books make clear, was more ambitious for his client than his client was for himself. In the meantime, Rove set up what became a lucrative business as a political and business consultant; he was particularly skillful at running direct-mail campaigns. Before long, he had reorganized Texas politics so thoroughly that the once-Democratic state became dominated by Republicans—almost all of them Rove clients—who held every statewide elective office.

According to both books, Rove's career as a political operator was marked from the beginning by "dirty tricks," which Rove once referred to as "pranks." He learned from Atwater, for example, the efficacy of whispering campaigns—spreading scurrilous charges by radio, organized phone calls, and "push-polls," which circulate a rumor through the wording of a question. Texas Governor Ann Richards, whom Bush successfully challenged in 1994, was said to be a lesbian; John McCain was rumored to be mentally unstable and the father of a black child. (The McCains had adopted an orphan from Bangladesh.) Rove's clients, including George W. Bush, have been able to stay aloof from such smears, protesting that they had nothing to do with them. In *Bush's Brain* Moore and Slater write:

> A Rove candidate was always able to honestly argue that he was running a clean, issues-oriented campaign because Rove stirred up the dirt without involving his client. He made phone calls to reporters, supplied documents, and produced third-party groups with damaging allegations. This approach, already a template for the modern electoral campaign, was refined by Rove with a new precision.

Rove sometimes blunders. Absorbed in his study of political statistics, he didn't see McCain gaining on Bush in New Hampshire until it was too late, and McCain beat him by eighteen points. Next came South Carolina and vengeance. But Rove was always confident that Bush would defeat the less well funded and well organized McCain. When it came to the general election, Rove made another mistake, predicting that

Bush would defeat Gore by six points; overconfident in the closing weeks, he allowed Bush to run a leisurely campaign and wasted the candidate's time and resources in California, where he had no chance of winning.

After the 2000 election, Rove not only became Bush's White House political adviser but effectively took over the Republican National Committee. Rove forced out his and Bush's first choice as chairman, former governor James Gilmore of Virginia, whom he didn't find compliant enough, and installed Mark Racicot, the former governor of Montana and a friend of Bush's, who had been very helpful during the Florida recount, making numerous television appearances pressing Bush's case. But in fact Rove runs the RNC through its deputy chairman, Jack Oliver, a longtime Bush family loyalist.

About a year before the 2000 election, Rove made an alliance with the anti-tax lobbyist Grover Norquist, probably the most influential figure in organizing the American right, without which Bush could not have become president and probably couldn't be reelected in 2004. Rove not only cultivates the right, the Republican Party's base, but through Norquist he is trying to broaden the constituencies he reaches. Both men are expert coalition builders, and together they are attempting to assemble a coalition to guarantee conservative Republican dominance of American politics.

They are going about it in several different ways. While the tax cuts that Bush—like Norquist—advocates favor the very rich, Rove and Norquist have also been concentrating on appeals to small businesses, which maintain one of the most powerful lobbies in Washington and whose owners have long wanted to abolish the estate tax (which Norquist has dubbed "the death tax"). That aim was accomplished in Bush's first tax bill, and small business also favors his new tax legislation. Rove and Norquist act on the assumption that stockholders, who currently are estimated to make up 50 percent of American households and 70 percent of voters (what Norquist terms "the investor class"), would favor Bush's proposal to eliminate the tax on dividends. (About the investor class, Norquist says, "Rove understands it.")

The two men also collaborate on getting more ethnic groups to vote Republican, not just Hispanics but also Muslims and immigrants from India and Pakistan—a large number of whom, Norquist observes, own small businesses. Rove has been closely following Norquist's efforts to expand the influence of his own coalition of groups on the right by installing branches of it in additional states. When the two men meet, which they do fairly frequently, Norquist shows Rove a map indicating where his state coalition groups exist—there are now thirty of them—and Rove has urged him to set up organizations in West Virginia, Missouri, and

North Carolina, all states important to Bush's reelection. "He keeps pushing," Norquist says. (Rove perceived that Bush could carry West Virginia, traditionally a Democratic state, in 2000; and, after an intensive effort involving not only television advertising but also three trips to the state by the candidate, two by Dick Cheney, and appearances by Bush's parents, as well as Charlton Heston, who received a hero's welcome, Bush won it. Moore and Slater write: "No decision Rove made in the 2000 general election more clearly illustrated his political genius.") Four times a year, Rove attends Norquist's Wednesday morning meetings with his allies in Washington, and he has held fund-raisers for Norquist's group.

Bush's campaign for president was hardly the first deceptive presidential campaign—FDR in 1932 pledged a balanced budget—but in hindsight its cynicism was astonishing. Having won the nomination with the strong help of the Republican Party's conservative base, and aware that elections in the US are won by attracting voters who are neither strongly liberal nor strongly conservative, Bush tacked toward the middle, especially for the cameras—there were several scenes, for example, showing him with black children. During the summer of 2000, when I remarked to Norquist that Bush was apparently "moving to the center," he quickly set me straight. Bush was doing just what the right wanted, he said: backing tax cuts, missile defense, privatization of social security, the "right to life," limits on punitive damages (or "tort reform"), and opposing gun control. Since the election, of course, Bush has governed from the right.

Rove has been promoting tort reform for years, and sees it as an effective political weapon. When he persuaded Bush to favor it in his first race for the Texas governorship, one of the clients of his consulting firm was Philip Morris. "I sort of talked him into that one," Rove said, according to *Boy Genius*. Moreover, Rove understood that the trial lawyers not only support the Democrats but also, having won large contingency fees, could make huge contributions to their favored candidates. It could help Republicans if those fees were diminished. Tort reform has now become a national Republican cause as well. Norquist says, "If you're a pro-business party you want to curb punitive damages."

In the 2002 midterm elections, Rove was more active than any White House adviser had ever been before. He was instrumental not only in selecting Senate candidates but also, as in the case of North Carolina's Elizabeth Dole, in discouraging others from running. He had done the same in Texas. From Rove's fertile imagination came the idea, months before the 2002 midterm elections, in which control of the Senate was at stake, to capitalize on the Senate Democrats' opposition to the part of the bill creating a Department of

Homeland Security which denied its employees traditional civil service protections. This was seen as a way to break the power of the public employees union, which supports the Democrats. Norquist believes that the union is a force for the expansion of government. Democrats who opposed the bill because of its anti-union provisions were branded "unpatriotic."

At first, it seemed absurd to make a critical campaign issue over a bill to create a new federal department. But Bush was willing to do so, and it testified to Rove's dark genius that the strategy worked. In a speech by Rove to the Republican National Committee in January 2002, he urged Republicans to take political advantage of Bush's war on terrorism, arguing that the public has more confidence in Republicans on national defense. There's reason to suspect that the resolution approving war against Iraq was deliberately timed by Rove and Bush to occur just before the 2002 midterm election.

The charge of a lack of patriotism helped to defeat Senator Max Cleland of Georgia, who had lost two legs and an arm in the Vietnam War. Of course it was outrageous to brand Cleland "unpatriotic," but Bush and Rove are not easily embarrassed. Bush, for all his supposedly easygoing manner, is apparently no less ruthless than his mentor. A television ad showed Cleland along with pictures of Osama bin Laden and Saddam Hussein. The Republican senator Chuck Hagel of Nebraska, himself a Vietnam veteran, was so incensed by the ad that he threatened to run his own ad endorsing Cleland unless it was canceled. After Hagel's vehement protests, it was, but the damage had been done.

Essentially the same ad was run against the South Dakota Democratic senator Tim Johnson, whose son had served in the military in Afghanistan and is currently serving in Iraq. Johnson won, but just barely. South Dakota has been a battleground for Bush and Rove since Tom Daschle, a native of the state, became majority leader of the Senate in 2001, and the midterm election in South Dakota became a proxy fight between Bush and Daschle. In November 2001, an ad was run showing Daschle, who was not up for reelection, next to a picture of Saddam Hussein. So much for Bush's 2000 campaign pledge to "change the tone" in Washington. The authors of Boy Genius make a persuasive case that Rove was well aware of the ads, and may have had a part in conceiving them. The Republicans retook the Senate in November 2002.

Bush's Brain portrays Rove as an implacable, unforgiving man who sees things in black and white. In a memo for a Texas client he once described his campaign strategy as "Attack. Attack. Attack." And according to Moore and Slater, Rove regards a political opponent or a rival consultant as someone who must be punished, if possible destroyed. (Rove is so competitive, the authors write, that his wife told

13

a reporter, "Even in croquet he'd be hitting my ball so far I was crying on vacation.")

Though John McCain has vigorously supported Bush on the wars in Afghanistan and Iraq, and on some other matters as well, he remains on the list of enemies. Political consultants and lobbyists who supported McCain in 2000 had to maneuver nimbly if they were to gain entrée into the Bush inner circle; few were able to do so. Several McCain supporters, some of them highly qualified, were barred from jobs in the Bush administration. After Congress passed McCain's campaign finance reform bill, Bush indulged in the petty act of signing it suddenly one morning, with only a few White House staff present. The same sort of pettiness led the White House to snub Vermont Senator Jim Jeffords and helped push him from the Republican side of the aisle to become an independent and vote with the Democrats, temporarily giving the Democrats control of the Senate and dealing a huge blow to Bush's program.

One disturbing aspect of the close working relationship between Bush and Rove is that each man is capable of deep and lasting resentments. Now that Karen Hughes, the other staff member who was probably as close to Bush as Rove is, has returned to Texas and only occasionally comes to Washington, there appears to be no one to interrupt the mutually reinforcing anger that runs between the two men.

Bush's resentments extend not just to political opponents but also to entire countries, not only France and Germany, but Turkey as well. (A former Clinton foreign policy adviser calls it "policy by snit.")

Bush and Rove were widely credited with having the audacity to risk political reversal and campaign hard in the 2002 midterm election—especially since their efforts succeeded: the Republicans gained two seats to retake the Senate, and increased their House majority by six seats, only the third time since the Civil War that the party holding the White House gained House seats in a midterm election. Yet the Republican victory was not as sweeping as the television commentators suggested on election night. In fact, several of the Senate races were very close—a shift of only 107,000 votes in Missouri, Minnesota, and New Hampshire would have kept the Senate in Democratic control—and some of the House victories could be attributed to reapportionments creating districts more favorable to Republicans. Moore and Slater argue, plausibly, that the strategy of Bush and Rove in 2002 was more a matter of necessity than audacity, because Bush needed the mandate that he didn't receive in 2000. But he is acting as if he received a larger mandate in 2002 than he did.

Since then, with Republican control of Congress, Bush dominates Washington, with Karl Rove by his side. And in Congress's agenda this year is their program for the 2004 election: another steep tax cut; a ban on "partial-birth abortion"; trapping the Democrats into opposing the nomination of a conservative Hispanic for an important judgeship; and tort reform.

Rove protests to outsiders that he's not involved in foreign policy, knowing that this would appear unseemly for a political consultant. But he does in fact take part in foreign policy decisions—as usual, from the perspective of what's in the President's electoral interests. This is probably the most tightly concealed aspect of his many activities. Press reports have documented his urging Bush to tilt his Middle East policy further toward Ariel Sharon—seeking to solidify Bush's support from the Christian right, which strongly favors a Greater Israel, and to increase Bush's share of the Jewish vote in 2004. Of course Rove wasn't alone in this view; he was joined in it by the group of conservatives and neoconservatives (including Dick Cheney, Donald Rumsfeld, and Paul Wolfowitz) who saw Israel as the only truly reliable ally in the Middle East. Less well known was Rove's intervention in a presidentially appointed mission to seek peace in Sudan. He urged negotiators to find a solution favoring the Christian forces in the south—which are supported by the Christian right— over their Muslim opponents who govern in the north.

One of the more striking indications of Rove's influence

on foreign policy may have occurred this year in a statement Bush made in his press conference on March 6, while he was still maneuvering to get the UN to approve a second resolution endorsing the imminent war in Iraq. Even if the resolution didn't have enough votes, Bush said, the members of the Security Council should vote because "it's time for people to show their cards." This recalled an incident from Rove's career while he was still a consultant in Texas, when he went ahead with what he knew would be a hostile hearing before a state senate committee, controlled by the Democrats, on his nomination to serve on the board of East Texas University. Though he knew that he would be rejected, he explained later, he had gone ahead with the hearing because "I was going to make them do it." Bush's vow to proceed with the UN vote was a blunder; he later had to go back on it.

Moore and Slater argue that Rove has been deeply involved in Bush's policy toward Iraq and it seems altogether likely that he has; but here they are on weaker ground than in other parts of the book because much of their case is based on surmise, and they also neglect the strong influence of Cheney, Rumsfeld, and Wolfowitz. Still, some aspects of Bush's handling of the matter have a Roveian ring. When Colin Powell was preparing his presentation to the UN Security Council on February 6, he resisted citing the alleged links between Iraq and al-Qaeda; he was forced to do so at the White

House's insistence. This was the weakest part of his presentation. It has not been established that Rove was involved in the decisions about Powell's speech; but it is a safe bet that he took the view that going to war with Iraq would have more public support if people thought that it was involved with the September 11 attack and that if officials said it often enough, the public would believe it. In fact, one poll published shortly before the war began showed that 42 percent of the American people believe that Iraq was involved in the attack.

Moore and Slater think that Rove is a dangerous man, but their book is not biased or malicious, based as it is on solid reporting (until they venture into the subject of Iraq). They worry about someone so single-mindedly dedicated to his employer's political success sitting in the White House with ready access to the instruments of power. It's hard to think of a precedent for this—apart from Richard Nixon's White House, with its "enemies list" which resulted in audited tax returns and other retaliatory actions. The authors of *Bush's Brain* quote a Washington consultant who works for both parties as saying that Rove is "Nixonian," and his political record prompts the thought that Rove is Bush's Nixon. Like Nixon, Rove sees enemies all around him; he is bent on vengeance and isn't averse to employing unscrupulous methods or exploiting patriotic emotions. His nearly unchecked power is disturbing—but Bush has to be held accountable for his actions.

More important than Rove's personal character, though, is that the brilliant visionary who, with manic energy, remade the politics of the state of Texas—recruiting candidates, throwing opponents on the defensive, raising vast amounts of money—is now trying to do the same thing to the nation.

As published in *The New York Review of Books*
June 12, 2003

THE NEOCONS IN POWER

THE CONFLICT WITHIN THE BUSH ADMINISTRATION in recent months over policy for postwar Iraq has caused much confusion and has already damaged the reconstruction effort. The stakes are enormous not just for the US and for the people of Iraq, but for the entire Middle East, and the rest of the world. Almost from the outset of the Bush administration there have been battles between the State Department and the Defense Department, but the controversy over postwar Iraq has brought out bitterness and knife-wielding of a sort that Washington has seldom seen.

To some extent, the tension between the two departments is inherent because of their different missions. This conflict spills over into the White House and the think tanks and the offices of various consultants around town. It is really a conflict between the neoconservatives, who are largely responsible for getting us into the war against Iraq, and those they disparagingly call the "realists," who tend to be more cautious about the United States' efforts to remake the Middle East into a democratic region.

The word "neoconservative" originally referred to former liberals and leftists who were dismayed by the countercultural movements of the 1960s and the Great Society, and adopted conservative views, for example, against government welfare programs, and in favor of interventionist foreign policies. A group of today's "neocons" now hold key positions in the Pentagon and in the White House and they even have a mole in the State Department.

The most important activists are Richard Perle, who until recently headed the Defense Policy Board (he's still a member), a once-obscure committee, ostensibly just an advisory group but now in fact a powerful instrument for pushing neocon policies; James Woolsey, who has served two Democratic and two Republican administrations, was CIA director during the Clinton administration, and now works for the management consulting firm Booz Allen Hamilton; Kenneth Adelman, a former official in the Ford and Reagan administrations who trains executives by using Shakespeare's plays as a guide to the use of power (www.moversandshake-speares.com); Paul Wolfowitz, the deputy secretary of defense and the principal advocate of the Iraq policy followed by the administration; Douglas Feith, the undersecretary of defense for policy, the Pentagon official in charge of the reconstruction of Iraq; and I. Lewis ("Scooter") Libby, Vice President Cheney's chief of staff. Two principal allies of this core group are John Bolton, undersecretary of state for arms control (though he opposes arms control) and international security affairs, and Stephen Hadley, the deputy national security adviser. Cheney himself and Defense Secretary Donald Rumsfeld can be counted as subscribing to the neocons' views about Iraq.

A web of connections binds these people in a formidable alliance. Perle, Wolfowitz, and Woolsey have long been close friends and neighbors in Chevy Chase, Maryland. The three have worked with one another in the Pentagon, served on the same committees and commissions, and participated in the same conferences. Feith is a protégé of Perle, and worked under him during the Reagan administration. Adelman, a friend of Perle, Wolfowitz, and Woolsey, is very close to Cheney and Rumsfeld. The Cheneys and the Adelmans share a wedding anniversary and celebrate it together each year; Adelman worked for Rumsfeld in three government positions, and the Adelmans have visited the Rumsfelds at their various homes around the country. Woolsey and Adelman are members of Perle's Pentagon advisory group. At the outset of this administration Perle made sure that it was composed of people who share his hawkish views. (Perle recently resigned the chairmanship over allegations of conflicts of interest with his private consulting business, but he remains a member of the advisory board, and his power isn't diminished.) Bolton, over the objections of Colin Powell, was appointed to the State Department at the urging of his neocon allies. (A State

Department official said to me recently, referring to the Pentagon, "Why don't we have a mole over there?")

Perle, Woolsey, and Wolfowitz are all disciples of the late Albert Wohlstetter, a University of Chicago professor who had worked for the RAND Corporation and later taught at the University of California. Throughout the cold war he argued that nuclear deterrence wasn't sufficient—that the US had to actually plan to fight a nuclear war in order to deter it. He strongly advocated the view that the military power of the USSR was underrated. Wolfowitz earned his Ph.D. under Wohlstetter; Perle met Wohlstetter when he was a high school student in Los Angeles and was invited by Wohlstetter's daughter to swim in their pool. Later, Wohlstetter invited Perle, then a graduate student at Princeton, to Washington to work with Wolfowitz on a paper about the proposed Anti-Ballistic Missile Treaty, which Wohlstetter opposed and which has been abandoned by the Bush administration. Wohlstetter introduced Perle to Democratic Senator Henry ("Scoop") Jackson of Washington, an aggressive cold warrior and champion of Israel's interests. Woolsey (who calls himself "a Scoop Jackson Democrat") came to know Wohlstetter in 1980, when they both served on a Pentagon panel. Of Wohlstetter Woolsey said in a conversation we had in mid-April, "A key to understanding how Richard and Paul and I think is Albert. He's had a major impact on us." And through Wohlstetter, Perle met

Ahmed Chalabi, then an Iraqi exile who had founded the Iraqi National Congress, an umbrella organization of Iraqi groups, many of its members in exile.

Perle's career has been an astonishing one. Though he has held only one government position—that of an assistant secretary of defense during the Reagan administration—he has had tremendous influence over the administration's Iraq policy. He openly advocated the overthrow of the Saddam Hussein regime shortly after he left the Pentagon in 1987. In the 1970s, while working on Jackson's Senate staff, he opposed détente, helped to stop ratification of the SALT II arms control agreement, and aided Jackson in getting through Congress the Jackson-Vanik law, which cut off trade with the Soviet Union if it continued to bar the emigration of Jews. During the Reagan administration, when he was assistant secretary of defense for policy, Perle became famous for opposing arms control agreements and acquired the nickname "The Prince of Darkness." Working with a small group of journalists who circulate his views, he's been known to savage someone he opposes on a big issue. He makes his influence felt through frequent television appearances, through his network of allies in the bureaucracy, and through his strategy of staking out an extreme position and trying to make the ground shift in his direction—which it often has. He is a strong advocate of the views of right-wing Israeli leaders, and serves on the board of the company that owns the pro-Likud *Jerusalem Post*. When he's not working with his clients, who include defense contractors, he is a resident fellow at the American Enterprise Institute, a conservative think tank. From this position Perle invites people to an annual conference in Beaver Creek, Colorado, cosponsored by AEI and former president Gerald Ford, and he has several times invited Ahmed Chalabi as his guest there. At the conferences, Chalabi was able to meet Cheney, Rumsfeld, and Wolfowitz.

Chalabi fled Iraq when he was thirteen, along with other members of his wealthy and prominent Shiite family, after the military coup in 1958 that overthrew the British-installed monarchy. He studied in America—earning an undergraduate degree in mathematics at MIT, and then a doctorate, also in mathematics, at the University of Chicago (where he met Wohlstetter)—and then went into banking. He has been tried and convicted, in absentia, in Jordan on charges of fraud and embezzlement over the collapse of the Petra Bank, which he founded and ran. (Chalabi has said that the bank's collapse was the result of a plot by Saddam Hussein's government.[1]) After founding the Iraqi National Congress in 1992, he received CIA funds. In 1995, working from Kurdish territory in northern Iraq, he promoted a coup against Saddam Hussein, but his plan fizzled. Even one of his current allies says he "may have over-stated" the degree of support his attempted coup would receive from disaffected members of the Iraqi military.

Chalabi claimed at the time that the CIA supported him, but Anthony Lake, then Clinton's national security adviser, denies this. "Fearing another Bay of Pigs," he told me, "everyone agreed that we needed to be crystal clear with Chalabi. The United States had already betrayed the Kurds twice, and we didn't want to see it happen again by our encouraging such a dubious operation. So I personally sent him a message that we didn't support him." A current senior administration official says that Saddam's government knew in advance about Chalabi's plan, and had penetrated it.

Back in Washington, where he spent a great deal of time, Chalabi impressed various members of Congress, among them John McCain and Joseph Lieberman, and was the moving force behind the passage in 1998 of the Iraq Liberation Act, which called for the overthrow of the Saddam regime and directed that the State Department grant $97 million to the INC. But before long the department, suspicious that the organization had misallocated funds, ordered an audit, announced "accounting irregularities," and held up further contributions—to the everlasting fury of Perle and other neocons. When the Bush administration came in, the Pentagon began funding the INC.

Chalabi's role in postwar Iraq has become one of the most contentious issues within the Bush administration. The State Department considers him "damaged goods," and someone who has been out of touch with Iraq for too long. The neocons admire him as a man of strong intelligence and a courageous fighter for the overthrow of Saddam and for democracy in Iraq; they see him as the perfect person to lead postwar Iraq. After the start of the war, without informing the State Department, the Pentagon flew Chalabi and his paramilitary forces, which the American military had trained in Hungary, back into Iraq. Their intention was to give him a strong head start toward becoming the leader of the new Iraqi government. But the State Department objected to the US installing Iraq's new leader, and Colin Powell argued strenuously in National Security Council meetings that the United States should not impose a new ruler on Iraq, a position that the President adopted during discussions in February with his national security advisers: Cheney, Condoleezza Rice, Rumsfeld, Powell, and George Tenet of the CIA. The official position of the US government became that the Iraqi people should decide the future of Iraq and that the future leaders should be drawn from Iraqis who had been both inside and outside the country during the Saddam regime. But there's a question of how many anti-Baathist leaders could survive in Iraq during Saddam's reign. The neocons argue that no one comparable to Konrad Adenauer or Václav Havel is likely to be found inside Iraq.

Despite the President's position, Chalabi's friends in Washington continue to back him strongly. A senior member of the administration says, "Their whole approach to life seems to be to get Mr. Chalabi in a position of authority." A well-informed official told me recently that in National Security Council meetings, "Nobody would argue against the point that there had to be insiders and outsiders. Some people in the administration wouldn't argue against that point but wouldn't accept it." This person said that Rumsfeld and Wolfowitz, along with their like-minded outsiders, took the position that "we're going to fight this war and we're going to install Chalabi."

The British government takes a skeptical view of Chalabi—who spent several of his exile years in London—and has so informed the Bush administration. Even those outside the neocons' circle who think well of Chalabi agree that it's been a major mistake for Chalabi's US supporters to make it so apparent that he's their man in Iraq. US forces are now providing protection for Chalabi in Baghdad.

Perle says of Chalabi, "He's an exceptional person, brilliant, with the disciplined mind of a mathematician. He's someone you want to talk to—deeply knowledgeable of the region, its history and culture." He adds, "One of the sources of opposition to Chalabi is the dictators of the countries around Iraq and the reason is obvious: he's going to fight for democracy and other peoples will want it." Woolsey said, "The State Department bureaucracy tilts pro-Saudi and anti-Chalabi. The key thing about Ahmed is not that he's a banker, not that he wears $2,000 suits, not that he's been in and out of Iraq since he was a teenager. I think that the key problem is that he's Shiite: the State bureaucracy has been used to Sunni powers in Saudi Arabia, Egypt, Iraq—pretty much everywhere in the Middle East." (Sixty percent of the Iraqi people are Shiite but there are as yet no signs that the secular Chalabi has the support of Shiite religious leaders in Iraq.) Woolsey added, "The State Department bureaucracy likes to get along with clients and the CIA likes to control things and Chalabi isn't controllable, he has his own views."

When we talked in April Kenneth Adelman told me, "The starting point is that conservatives now are for radical change and the progressives—the establishment foreign policy makers—are for the status quo." He added, "Conservatives believe that the status quo in the Middle East is pretty bad, and the old conservative belief that stability is good doesn't apply to the Middle East. The status quo in the Middle East has been breeding terrorists."

IN JANUARY, THE PRESIDENT SIGNED A SECRET National Security Policy Directive, giving the Defense Department the authority to manage postwar policy in Iraq, and directing other agencies to coordinate with Defense. But this didn't settle things: conflict between the Defense Department and the State Department continued. The State Department submitted a list of people to serve in the reconstruction and the Defense Department rejected some of them without informing State.

2.

The appointment of retired general James Garner to run the reconstruction effort in Iraq was controversial from the outset. Garner was a friend of Rumsfeld from the days when they served together in 1998 on a commission that strongly advocated missile defense. After the first Gulf War Garner was much praised in northern Iraq for his management of Operation Provide Comfort, a program of aid for Kurdish refugees. The Bush I administration had urged the Kurds in northern Iraq, as well as the Shiites in southern Iraq, to rise against the Saddam regime, but then abandoned them. Garner, the president of a company that supplies missile parts, had advised Israel on the use of the Patriot missile during the Gulf War. More recently he was one of forty-four retired military officers who signed a document praising the "remarkable restraint" of Israel's defense forces "in the face of lethal violence orchestrated by" the PLO. Garner's support of Israel's government has been widely noted in the Arab press; the American conservative Jewish publication *Forward* in late March proudly published a piece headlined "Pro-Israel General Will Oversee Reconstruction of Postwar Iraq."

Before the war ended, Garner and a staff of a few hundred people installed themselves in a row of beachfront villas in Kuwait, and, in the deepest secrecy, made plans for the postwar period. After they got to Baghdad, they remained largely inaccessible in a grand palace, trapped by the insecure surroundings which they hadn't adequately planned for.

Then, in early May, came word that a civilian, Paul Bremer, a former State Department official in charge of counterterrorism and former manager of Henry Kissinger's consulting firm, would be installed as head of the reconstruction effort over Garner. The administration had become aware—belatedly—that it wasn't brilliant public relations to have a military man in charge of the reconstruction effort and that it was running into serious difficulties. US officials had failed to anticipate the degree of chaos that followed the war: they didn't have an adequate plan, didn't protect hospitals and other public buildings from looters, or citizens from violent crime, and by early May still hadn't restored many basic services. The leaders of long-repressed Shiite Muslims were taking charge of some neighborhoods and calling for a theocratic state. Iraqis were agitating for the US to leave. The State Department had argued from the outset that a civilian should run the reconstruction efforts, and the British government, among others, had complained to the Bush administration about the appointment of a military man.

Rumsfeld, I was told, suggested the appointment of Bremer, who is close to the neocons, and State Department officials were pleased with the idea because they considered Bremer, a former foreign service officer, to be one of them. Thus, Bremer's appointment was a rarity: State and Defense were both enthusiastic—while Garner was highly displeased and is to leave Iraq soon, along with some of the officials who were found lacking in skills needed for the postwar administration. But Robert Oakley, a former ambassador to Pakistan and Zaire, a special envoy to Somalia for two presidents, a former head of the counterterrorism program (he was succeeded by Bremer), and now a visiting fellow at the National Defense University, said to me after the shake-up, "I don't think it matters who's leaving and who's taking their place. It's too late. In large part events are developing out there in ways that may now be beyond our control."

Perle confirmed to me what others had told me—that he has been the leader of the pro-Chalabi group. "It may have been because I knew him longer and introduced him to others," he said. He has known Chalabi for twelve years. It was Chalabi who encouraged the US planners of the war to believe that the Shiites in the south would welcome the US forces as liberators (despite the fact that the US had betrayed them in 1991), that the Iraqi army would lack the will to fight, and that there would be substantial defections by the Republican Guard. This advice led Cheney to say on *Meet the Press*, "I really do believe that we will be greeted as liberators. . . . I think the regular army will not [fight, and that] significant elements of the Republican Guard are likely as well to want to avoid conflict"; and it led Kenneth Adelman to predict that defeating Saddam Hussein's regime would be a "cakewalk." The overconfidence of US officials was the result not only of Chalabi's "information" but also of their and Chalabi's eagerness to sell the war. Perle concedes having underestimated the role of the Fedayeen Saddam, a paramilitary force set up by Saddam's son Uday after the Gulf War. "What we didn't expect," Perle said, "was that the Fedayeen Saddam got moved south, by the busload"—thus causing the taking of some southern towns to be more difficult than expected.

Perle and Chalabi had argued that between 40,000 and 80,000 American soldiers would suffice, that if a small number of troops were sent in they could be augmented by forces recruited by the INC, and that large parts of the Iraqi military would quickly join them. As Rumsfeld began planning for an invasion, he ordered, as one option, a study for a war strategy using 80,000 troops. He was eager to prove his point that the military, in particular the Army, could be slimmed down, that many of its previous roles in combat could be performed by sophisticated new weapons and by Special Operations forces.

In holding down the number of US forces to fight in Iraq to approximately 230,000 to 250,000—roughly half the number of troops that were sent to fight in the Gulf War—and belatedly redirecting the troops that had been supposed to be sent through Turkey (they didn't arrive until after the fighting had ceased), Rumsfeld took some big chances. Among other consequences, there weren't enough troops to deal with the chaos in Baghdad after it fell to the allies. Some military experts also argue that supply lines were unnecessarily endangered, and that lives were unnecessarily lost. Retired General Wesley Clark said on CNN, "We took the risk and it worked out.... But I'm still of the school that would say, don't take risks if you don't have to take the risk." Rumsfeld has tried to have it both ways. In a single press briefing, he insisted both that there were adequate troops and that the Baghdad Museum couldn't be protected (though the Oil Ministry was) because "when some of that looting was going on, people were being killed, people were being wounded."

Rumsfeld's determination to hold down the number of

troops in Iraq carried over from the war to the postwar period. Earlier this year, General Eric Shinseki, the Army Chief of Staff, testified to Congress that at least 200,000 troops would be needed after the fighting ended. Rumsfeld and Wolfowitz, loath to have the public think that waging war in Iraq would impose a long-term burden on the US, were angered by Shinseki's testimony, which the next day Wolfowitz called "wildly off the mark." So then they were stuck with staying below 200,000 troops in Iraq. Rumsfeld rejected requests to have a sizable number of military police ready to impose order and protect facilities when the fighting ended. As of May 12, there were roughly 150,000 US troops inside Iraq, with many more in the region. Of late, officials have privately admitted that they underestimated the degree of lawlessness and looting that would follow the fighting—but this kind of activity has had many precedents in postwar situations.

Like Perle, Wolfowitz had favored bringing down the Saddam regime since before the Bush administration took office, and in meetings of the President's national security advisers just after September 11, Rumsfeld and Wolfowitz put forward their view that Saddam's regime should be eliminated. Iraq was a terrorist state, they argued, and should be made a target of the "war on terrorism." Kenneth Adelman says, "At the beginning of the administration people were talking about Iraq but it wasn't doable. There was no heft. That changed with September 11 because then people were willing to confront the reality of an international terrorist network, and terrorist states such as Iraq. The terrorist states are even worse than terrorist networks because they have so many more resources at their disposal—they have money, they have weapons, and they can send contraband material in diplomatic pouches."

Iraq's supposed ties to al-Qaeda have still not been proved; but Bush apparently became convinced that they existed. (Rumsfeld and Wolfowitz, unhappy that the CIA and the Pentagon's own Defense Intelligence Agency weren't confirming their charges about Iraq's ties to terrorist groups, set up their own intelligence group, one more likely to tell them what they wanted to hear.) By repeating the charge that Iraq was linked with international terrorism, the President and other officials succeeded in convincing nearly half the US public before the war that Iraq was involved in the attack on the World Trade Center. Several sources told me that if Cheney and his neocon allies had had their way, the war with Iraq would have begun in the fall of 2002; they attribute the delay to Powell's success in convincing Bush to take his case to the UN and send weapons inspectors to Iraq.

Not long after September 11, high US military officials

ELIZABETH DREW

were told by members of the Bush administration that the
regimes of six other countries besides Iraq would eventually
have to be removed because they harbored terrorist groups:
Syria, Iran, Lebanon, Somalia, Sudan, and Libya. The administration had declared a "war on terrorism," but, unsure how
to fight it, adopted the strategy of "draining the swamps" in
which it was said to breed. In announcing on May 1 the end
of "major combat" in Iraq, Bush called that war "one victory
in a war on terror that began on September 11, 2001, and
still goes on."

The neocons' assurance that the United States could not only
remove Saddam Hussein but also convert Iraq and the rest of
the Middle East into democratic nations relies on several false
analogies. Wolfowitz, his neocon allies, and the journalists
who circulate their ideas often cite Germany and Japan after
the Second World War as examples of countries that were
transformed into democracies. But unlike Iraq, Japan had a
largely homogeneous culture and a symbol of national unity,
the Emperor, who kept his title if not his power. Japan, in any
case, has had essentially one-party rule since the end of the
war. And Germany, which also had a cohesive society, had a
democratic constitution and parliamentary institutions until
Hitler was barely elected chancellor in 1933. Moreover, the
US occupied Japan for seven years and Germany for four.

Rumsfeld has said that no time limit can be set on the US occupation of Iraq, but US officials are aware that the longer it goes on the greater will be the danger to US troops there— and perhaps domestic pressures to bring them home. (The neocons—as well as officials of previous administrations and some academics—also assert that democracies don't make war on each other, but this is a highly debated proposition.)

Because some—but certainly not all—of the neoconservatives are Jewish and virtually all are strong supporters of the Likud Party's policies, the accusation has been made that their aim to "democratize" the region is driven by their desire to surround Israel with more sympathetic neighbors. Such a view would explain the otherwise puzzling statements by Wolfowitz and others before the war that "the road to peace in the Middle East goes through Baghdad." But it is also the case that Bush and his chief political adviser Karl Rove are eager both to win more of the Jewish vote in 2004 than Bush did in 2000 and to maintain the support of the Christian right, whose members are also strong supporters of Israel. The neoconservatives are powerful because they are cohesive, determined, ideologically driven, and clever (even if their judgment can be questionable), and some high administration officials, including the vice-president, are sympathetic to them. (Rove is known to have bought the road-through-Baghdad argument, which gave them a powerful boost.)

But the neocons don't win all the time. In the argument over how involved the UN should be in postwar Iraq, the State Department and Tony Blair favored a fairly large role whereas the Defense Department preferred virtually none at all. The President came down somewhere near the middle, saying that the UN should have a "vital" role. On May 9, the US circulated a draft resolution providing for a United Nations "special coordinator" who would work with the US on humanitarian activities and help US administrators in setting up political and civic institutions. Colin Powell is skilled in bureaucratic infighting, yet when the White House makes a decision that favors Powell, the ideologues on the right don't take this as final: they keep pushing. Powell's general inclination, after he has fought for a position, is to support his commander in chief—as he did on going to war in Iraq. A diplomatic source has called Powell "The Unsackable," because of his national popularity rating (higher than Bush's) and his international standing.

Rumsfeld was reported to be in trouble before September 11 for having alienated almost everyone—Congress, the military, defense contractors (who are big campaign contributors to the Republicans)—and his ideas for restructuring the military were going nowhere. He has been riding high since the war. On the Sunday after Baghdad fell, The *Washington Post* and

The *New York Times* ran front-page stories saying that Rumsfeld was now in a commanding position within the government. This was no accident. The stories were apparently encouraged by Rumsfeld's people. Rumsfeld and his associates saw the victory in Iraq as providing leverage for his struggles with other agencies and support for his program to change the military. So now Rumsfeld is "unsackable," too. As a result, as long as Powell and Rumsfeld choose to remain in place, the conflicts between the two departments—unprecedented in their intensity and openness—will go on.

Bush, who can by several accounts be snappish and harsh with his staff, even his highest-placed advisers (and has a fearsome temper), hates leaks and tolerates no open disagreement among advisers in other matters. He has fired some members of his administration for raising questions about his policies, in particular his economic program; yet he tolerates open conflict among his national security team. Some people argue that Condoleezza Rice should foster greater cooperation, but a former high State Department official says, "You can't coordinate people who refuse to be coordinated." The President himself seems unable or unwilling to impose order. People familiar with how Rumsfeld operates say that he cows people, makes them ill at ease in his presence; a former Republican official calls him "unsettling." Powell, for his part, raised questions about the planning for the war in meetings of the national security advisers, but said nothing publicly about his doubts. He has told people, "I'm no longer a soldier. I'm not going to manage defense policy." Rumsfeld has no corresponding reluctance about foreign affairs. In his virtually daily televised briefings—unprecedented for a cabinet officer—on which he clearly thrives, he has unhesitatingly insulted other countries, France and Germany among them.

The problems in a postwar Iraq were always going to be difficult, but they have been made worse as a result of several factors: the administration's zeal—particularly on the part of the neocons and their allies—to remove Saddam Hussein from power while failing to plan for the peace; Bush's pretense that he hadn't decided to go to war long after he apparently had in fact decided to; the administration's relative lack of interest in peacekeeping and belief that such efforts are politically unpopular (a carryover from the 2000 campaign that is also proving destructive in Afghanistan); and Rumsfeld's determination to hold down the number of troops in Iraq after the war—at whatever cost.

Senator Richard Lugar, the Republican chairman of the Senate Foreign Relations Committee, has publicly complained that the planning for the aftermath of the war "started very late.... A gap has occurred, and that has brought some suffering." Bush, whose presidency has been audacious and even radical, is now embarked on his riskiest gamble so far.

—May 14, 2003

FOOTNOTE

1 According to the London *Guardian* of April 14, "Reports compiled . . . by investigators in London and Jordan, including investigations by the accountants Arthur Andersen, describe how millions of dollars of depositors' money [in the Petra Bank] was transferred to other parts of the Chalabi family empire in Switzerland, Lebanon and London, and not repaid."

As published in *The New York Review of Books*
February 12, 2004

HUNG UP IN WASHINGTON

Like No Other Time:
The 107th Congress and the Two Years
That Changed America Forever
by Tom Daschle,
with Michael D'Orso.
Crown, 292 pp., $25.00

AS THE NATION HEADS TOWARD THE NOVEMBER ELECTIONS, it is now equally divided between the parties just as it was in 2000, but there are some important differences. George W. Bush's radical presidency has united the Democratic Party more closely than at any time since the end of World War II. True, Democrats solidly opposed Barry Goldwater, but not with the same animus. And Goldwater wasn't an incumbent president. Bush in 2000 convinced many Americans, including most of the pundits, that he would govern moderately. (Those who had talked to leaders of the right knew differently.) In recent elections, environmentalists and those favoring abortion rights mainly supported the Democrats but perhaps as many as a third of them voted Republican. In 2004 such "swing voters" are more likely to turn out for the Democratic nominee—although that of course depends on who that person is.

Many people have learned—or should have learned—from the 2000 election that their votes can matter. The hijacking of Florida produced a lasting anger that will probably energize the Democratic "base," those committed party members who are most likely to vote. (When Democratic candidates mention Florida, they unfailingly receive loud cheers and whistles.) If Ralph Nader chooses to run, that would of course complicate matters for the Democrats. But it seems doubtful that as many people will make the mistake of voting for him again in the belief that their vote doesn't matter.

The pollster John Zogby, who first predicted that the 2000 election would be a tie, says that he now foresees that each of the two major parties' candidates will get 45 percent of the vote in November, with the remaining 10 percent undecided. Zogby points out that while there was much talk of a Republican sweep of both houses of Congress in 2002, several of the Senate elections were actually quite close, and many voters made up their minds on election morning. The Republicans now control the Senate and the House by narrow margins. Congress, therefore, reflects the country at large: essentially evenly divided, and, like the base of each party, highly partisan and more than a little angry.

That, at least, is how things look now, early in 2004. But politics can change radically within even a few days. Sweeping theories are at best tenuous. In the late Sixties we were told about "The Emerging Republican Majority," and more recently we've had "The Emerging Democratic Majority." There is a certain refusal to accept that politics may depend on shifting factors and situations: the quality of the candidates, the impact of immediate events, and the atmosphere of the times. Would Richard Nixon have been elected in 1968 (thus setting off that emerging Republican majority and theories about "conservative realignment" in the US) if Lyndon Johnson had ended the Vietnam War by then, or even imposed a convincing bombing pause in time to help Hubert Humphrey? (As it was, George Wallace received 13.5 percent of the vote, while Nixon won by 1 percent.) The 1980 election supposedly demonstrated a "swing to the right," but it was a virtual tie going into the final weekend before the voting—and then Jimmy Carter, despite promises he had been given to the contrary and the expectations of success, failed to get the American hostages held in Iran released. Had he succeeded, there may well not have been a Republican sweep. Several Democratic senators were defeated by far smaller margins than those by which Reagan won their states.

The close division of Congress, in these times of vital questions about war, about economic policy, about equity in tax and social policy, about our natural resources, even about the very nature of government, has led to a new and more intense level of partisanship. Beyond that, the current division has brought about institutional changes, which, should they become permanent, are adverse to the future of democracy itself.

A timely new book by Senate Minority Leader Tom Daschle, *Like No Other Time: The 107th Congress and the Two Years That Changed*

America Forever, reveals a great deal about the period we have just been through and, unlike most books by politicians, is well written and highly readable. Daschle, who is in his third term in the Senate and previously served in the House, is a liberal Democrat from South Dakota, who became Senate majority leader in 1994, beating the gregarious and popular Christopher Dodd of Connecticut by one vote. This event in itself suggested that the seemingly mild-mannered Daschle has a far tougher inner core than is apparent on the surface. A prairie-state liberal, not quite as much a populist as his North Dakota colleagues and friends Byron Dorgan and Kent Conrad, Daschle also has a pragmatic streak that leads him to make compromises with the Republican administration—as when he ended up, after considerable agonizing, supporting the resolution authorizing Bush to use force in Iraq. (Daschle had earlier tried unsuccessfully to encourage Joseph Biden and Richard Lugar to formulate a more limited resolution.)

Daschle often has a difficult time trying to get Democratic senators, who are notably independent and even mulish, to follow him. (Republicans are by nature more cohesive, perhaps because they are more apt to respect authority.) He has a canny instinct for understanding complex Senate rules, yet sometimes he disappoints his Democratic colleagues by not exerting stronger leadership. But that may now be impossible for Senate leaders. In this age of politicians who largely raise their own funds and are much concerned, even fearful, about pleasing their own constituencies, Lyndon Johnson would never get away with his strong-arm tactics.

Daschle is sometimes too nice for his own good. It is clear from talking to him that he still has a hard time accepting the reality that when the war resolution was before Congress, Dick Gephardt, then the House minority leader, with whom he worked quite closely, betrayed him by going to the White House, without a word to him, and, in a Rose Garden ceremony that also included Joseph Lieberman, stood by while the President declared a compromise that amounted to a victory for himself.

In his book, Daschle describes the odd result of the 2000 election, when the Senate was evenly divided and the two parties shared power, with Vice President Dick Cheney breaking the tie votes. Then, in May of 2001, Jim Jeffords of Vermont switched from being a Republican to being an Independent who would vote with the Democrats, thus giving them control once again. Jeffords made his decision after strenuous behind-the-scenes negotiations in which both parties tried to gain a majority in the Senate. Over a period of months, Daschle had strongly encouraged Jeffords to make the switch, and at the same time he tried to encourage Republicans John McCain and Lincoln Chafee, a freshman from Rhode Island, to leave the Republican Party. Concurrently,

Republicans were trying to convince the conservative Democrat Zell Miller of Georgia to switch parties. Daschle describes McCain and Chafee as seeming "open at least to an invitation," but in the end, of course, they stayed Republican. Jeffords's decision caused an earthquake on Capitol Hill: there's little as shattering there as losing power, or as exhilarating as gaining it. The size of staffs and offices, and committee assignments, are all affected.

Not long after Jeffords's defection, however, the 2002 elections gave Bush control of all three branches of the government. The Democrats must now struggle to gain a majority of votes in the House and Senate by winning over some Republican moderates, or, in the Senate, by filibustering or threatening to. (It takes sixty votes to break a filibuster.) The Democrats don't often win a vote in the Senate, and when they do, it tends to be a vote on procedural matters. Referring to moderate Republicans, a Democratic senator says, "They're never with us when we really need them."

At the same time many Democrats, especially in the Senate, live in fear of Bush and his unscrupulous political strategist, Karl Rove.[1] Both men have demonstrated that they can be utterly ruthless, especially by questioning their Democratic opponents' patriotism. In 2002, they approved Republican ads showing Democratic senators' faces alongside those of

Saddam Hussein and Osama bin Laden. Such an ad was run against Daschle after he became Senate majority leader in 2001, though he wasn't up for reelection until 2004. He is now a major White House target.

The combination of near unity on the part of Republicans and fear among Democrats has rendered Congress essentially passive toward the President's foreign policy. It has paid scant attention to embarrassing and dangerous intelligence failures and enabled the President to lie about the reasons for going to war in Iraq. It has produced a tax code heavily slanted toward the rich, and enacted an appalling new Medicare law.

2.

AT A TIME WHEN FUNDAMENTAL QUESTIONS FACE THE COUNTRY, even about the very nature of government, the closely divided Congress has led to a new level of partisanship.

Between the 2002 elections and the Republicans' officially taking control of the Senate the following January, the Majority Leader Trent Lott, after making a racially tinged "joke" about Strom Thurmond, was forced out of his job, which was then filled by Bill Frist, a heart surgeon from Tennessee. Frist's polite, considerate manner and the difficulty he has encountered from some of Lott's allies are central to understanding how the Senate has—or has not—dealt with matters critical to the nation since 2002.

Like Daschle's, Frist's mild demeanor masks toughness and ambition. Though conservative, he's closer to the center than the other powerful Senate leaders—including Pennsylvania's Rick Santorum, whose rude behavior and sometimes wild rhetoric make him perhaps the most obnoxious member of the Senate[2]; John Kyl, of Arizona; and Don Nickles, of Oklahoma. They are all more familiar than Frist is with the Senate rules and sometimes outmaneuver him on tactics, thereby adding to the partisan atmosphere. So, though the Senate appears on the surface to be a calmer place than it was before Frist took over, that's deceptive.[3]

In dealing with the nation's business, the House has long been more partisan (and rowdy) than the Senate, the big change coming after the Republicans, led by the radical Newt Gingrich, took over the House in 1994. Though Gingrich has since been replaced by the milder-mannered Dennis Hastert of Indiana, the House is essentially run by the Republican whip, Tom DeLay. (Gingrich's overzealousness caused the Republicans to lose a number of House seats in 1998. He ran ads on the Monica Lewinsky affair even after Clinton had been impeached and at a time when there were far more pressing issues facing the country. And so the Republicans forced him out.)[4]

DeLay, the mean-spirited partisan from Texas, has extended his influence from Capitol Hill to the lobbying and law firms in downtown Washington, insisting that they hire more Republicans or, in the case of some trade associations, that they be headed by a Republican. DeLay is unforgiving and he has the troops to enforce his will. Christopher Shays, a moderate Republican from Connecticut, was denied a committee chairmanship because he had defied the House leadership by co-sponsoring the McCain-Feingold campaign finance bill, which was signed into law in 2002.

DeLay's zeal has had the effect of further polarizing the House along party lines, with the result that major legislation, from airline safety to expansion of Medicare, has been held up or passed only after the leadership or the White House exerted extraordinary pressures on reluctant Republicans.

ELIZABETH DREW

Reaching compromise on the final form of legislation even
with Senate Republicans has been difficult. The increasing
unwillingness to compromise is not only blocking legislation
but, it is not overdramatic to say, is subverting fundamental
concepts of democracy. The people's business is not getting
done. How can this happen if these representatives have to
face their constituents every two years?

One answer lies in the frequent redistricting of House
seats, in which both parties collude, and which has put more
and more House seats out of contention. In each election, the
number of contested House seats drops. In 2002, only
between twenty-two and twenty-five out of the 435 House
seats, or 5 percent, were genuinely contested. The result, Jim
Jaffe, who previously worked on Capitol Hill, wrote recently
in the *Chicago Tribune*, is that the very idea of democracy is
being threatened. "By acting... to create districts in which a
single party has an overwhelming majority," Jaffe wrote,
members of Congress "protect their jobs and make voting in
general elections an empty exercise." The increasing number
of safe seats makes fewer and fewer members interested in
compromise.

In his book, Daschle reveals several things we hadn't known.
He gives us a better sense than we had before of the chaos on
Capitol Hill on September 11: there was a warning from the

54

Capitol Police that a plane was headed toward the Capitol, bent on destroying it. The nation's leaders there, ostensibly "plugged into some top-secret, high-tech source of instant information," were in fact "as utterly clueless as everyone else." The fire alarm system was never activated, so many people who worked in the Capitol didn't know that an evacuation was taking place. There was complete confusion about where the senators were supposed to go. Some simply went home through the jammed traffic; some were finally directed to a decrepit building near the Capitol which housed the Capitol Police. There they watched in horror the television replays of the destruction of the two World Trade Center buildings and the attack on the Pentagon. Congressional leaders, unable to agree where they should go next, simply scattered, but then they were collected and evacuated by helicopter to one of the government's several underground "relocation centers"—Daschle of course can't tell us where —constructed during the cold war and containing desks, cubicles, and television monitors. That evening, after a heated debate about what they should do, they returned to the Capitol.

Daschle gives us a particularly telling account of what happened when envelopes containing deadly anthrax spores were delivered to his office, as well as the offices of two other senators. This was no "scare," as it was frequently described at the time. It was a horror. Dozens of lives were at risk; squabbling federal agencies delayed delivery of the right medicine. The victims and their families were left in ignorance about what to do in this life-threatening situation. Daschle still doesn't know who sent the anthrax; nor, apparently, does the FBI.

Daschle also tells us that he was troubled by the breadth of Bush's declaration in his talk at the National Cathedral on September 14, 2001, that he would "rid the world of evil." Daschle found it "a disturbingly unfocused and ill-defined mission, if ever there was one," and he objected to Bush's continual use of the word "evil." But these concerns, he writes, were subsumed "by the inspiration and pride" he felt in Bush's performance that day.

He also writes of the way the USA Patriot Act, which was passed in the sweep of emotion after September 11 and gave law enforcement agencies broad new powers, was modified by the Senate. The principal change required that the act be "sunset," i.e., it would be reevaluated by the Congress after four years. But Daschle doesn't give a clear sense of what is still wrong with the law even as modified. He fails to point out, for example, that it permits searches and seizures without a judicial warrant, authorizes surveillance of public libraries, and prevents Congress from overseeing how it is implemented.

Daschle displays unusually intense fury with Bush for saying in the autumn of 2002 that Democrats who were holding up the bill to create a Department of Homeland Security
were "not interested in the security of the American people."
Many Democrats opposed provisions of the bill that were
intended to carry out the administration's longstanding goal
of destroying civil service unions, which tend to back
Democrats. What followed was the smear campaign against
the Vietnam veteran Max Cleland and others who opposed
those provisions: a Republican-sponsored ad showed a picture of Cleland, who had lost three limbs in Vietnam, alongside pictures of bin Laden and Hussein. He was defeated.

Fierce Senate partisanship was also evident in the bitter fights
over Bush's conservative nominations to the federal courts,
which culminated in November of 2003 in a Republican filibuster that achieved nothing. The Republicans were in effect
filibustering themselves, holding up their own legislation. A
number of Republican senators were unhappy because, they
argued, Democrats on the Judiciary Committee were,
through various means, blocking Bush's nominations. But it
was a phony issue. In fact, according to committee sources,
when the Democrats invoked a rule requiring that at least
one minority member of the committee agree that it vote
on a nomination, this rule was ignored by the committee

chairman, Orrin Hatch. In fact, only a half-dozen have been blocked by Democrats in the committee. All but six of the 175 Bush nominations that reached the floor were approved; the rest were blocked by filibuster. Yet Bush, who shows little patience with the "advise and consent" role of the Senate, and some of the more conservative senators, including Santorum and Nickles, believed that the Republicans weren't getting enough political advantage from making an issue over the blocked nominations, and so they decided on the filibuster. By contrast, during Clinton's presidency, the Republicans held up more than sixty judicial nominees. Either way, the nomination system for federal judges has broken down.

Extreme partisanship also strongly affected major legislation in the 2003 session of Congress. The Medicare bill adopted by Congress and signed into law by Bush was put across by the drug and insurance industries, both of which have contributed a great deal of money to elected politicians, in particular to Republicans, and have strong influence on Capitol Hill. In amounting to a step toward the privatization of Medicare, a major goal (along with privatizing Social Security) of Bush and the right, the bill has been inspired by ideology as well as by the influence of money. It does nothing to deal with the fact that Medicare will be bankrupt in a decade, and will require a sizable increase in taxes to pay for it or a substantial paring back of benefits. The new prescription drug benefit included in the Medicare bill, minuscule when it is measured against the need, is a victim of the budget deficit, the Iraq war, and conservative ideologues who balk at establishing a new entitlement program. The bill also does nothing to lower the costs of drugs; on the contrary, it actually prohibits the federal government from bargaining over prices of drugs and other medical supplies and makes it extremely difficult for citizens to purchase American-made drugs at the lower prices at which they are available in Canada and other countries. Nor does the new drug benefit cover the middle class.

The White House tried to mitigate the negative political impact of seniors' discovering what's actually in the bill. It postponed implementing the new prescription drug program until 2006, while enabling seniors to purchase drug-discount cards before the 2004 election—even if they are useless for two years. Nevertheless, many older citizens have learned what's in the new law, and they're furious with the Republicans, as Democrats had hoped, as well as with the AARP (formerly called the American Association for Retired People) for going along with the drug companies and the insurers, with which the AARP does business.

Republicans allowed no House Democrats and only two Senate Democrats, Max Baucus and John Breaux, both of whom supported the Medicare bill, to participate in the House–Senate conference setting its final terms. It had been passed by the House by a five-vote margin (220–215) just before 6:00 AM, after the Republican leaders made extraordinary efforts to persuade reluctant members—a process that took three hours rather than the usual fifteen minutes for a roll-call vote. Republican House leaders made offers of campaign funds to reluctant conservatives; they also threatened one Republican, who was planning to retire, with cutting off money for his son, who was running to replace him. This sort of rough stuff is without recent precedent.

When the House was working on an energy bill last year, Democrats weren't even given a room in which to meet to draft an alternative, and Democrats were excluded from the House–Senate negotiations. The final bill failed in the Senate because liberals felt that it was too generous toward energy companies, and fiscal conservatives felt that it contained too much "pork." Frist couldn't get enough votes to end a filibuster against it. Many senators opposed the bill's provision granting immunity from lawsuits to manufacturers of a gasoline additive (methyl tertiary-butyl ether, or MTBE) that pollutes water. Once again, there seemed no possibility of compromise on a vital issue.

ONE OF THE MYSTERIES OF THE 2004 ELECTION is how large a part money will have in determining the next president. President Bush has amassed about $100 million and is aiming for an unprecedented $200 million. As in 2000, he's rejecting federal matching funds, which would require limits on spending. So are John Kerry and Howard Dean. Thus, the campaign finance law, the central reform put in place after Watergate, that specifically provides federal matching funds for presidential campaigns, has been weakened severely, if not fatally. Partly as a result, some candidates will have far more money available for campaign advertising and other activities, such as getting out the vote, than others. Still, though much is made of the importance of ads in political campaigns there's no way to precisely measure their impact. The pollsters, consultants, and ad producers, who stand to make many millions of dollars, nevertheless warn their clients that they must run a large number of ads or lose the election.

Bush has never liked the idea of campaign finance reform, though he had to pretend to during the 2000 primaries (when John McCain was challenging him) and when the campaign finance reform bill was going through Congress under McCain's leadership. But he tried to undermine McCain's efforts to pass the bill. In fact, few elected officials favor reform, but many of them feel they have to pretend that they do because of the strength of the reform movement

3.

among swing voters. Nevertheless, they try, through devious maneuvers, to weaken or even kill the legislation as it moves through Congress.

The ruling of the Supreme Court in December upholding the McCain-Feingold law passed by Congress in 2002 was of great consequence, even though it didn't require changes in the way the candidates were conducting their campaigns because the new law had already gone into effect in November 2002. (Bush signed it into law reluctantly and even secretly, excluding McCain from the signing in March 2002.) The law abolished "soft money"—unlimited contributions to candidates by individuals, corporations, or labor unions —and placed some curbs on broadcast ads that are called "issue" ads but that in fact attack candidates. The new law barred the use of corporate or union funds to pay for such ads thirty days before a primary and sixty days before an election.

Still, under the new law, "issue" ads can be paid for by aggregating "hard money"—individual donations by contributors of $2,000—or by a political action committee, or PAC, to which contributions of $5,000 can be made. There is no limit on the amount of "hard money" a PAC can spend for such ads. But there are various limits on the total amount individuals can donate to campaigns for federal office in each electoral cycle. The law also makes it illegal for federal officeholders to raise soft money.

In upholding the law, the Court rejected the impassioned argument of opponents of reform that the new law (and virtually every campaign finance reform law) infringed the First Amendment because, so it was argued, in making donations, citizens were exercising their right of free speech. Some who opposed the law and earlier bills on constitutional grounds were expressing a sincerely held view; for others the constitutional argument has been a useful cover for opposing any limits on raising or spending campaign money or on curbing bogus "issue" ads that are actually ads attacking a candidate, sometimes with mysterious funding.

The curb on broadcasting was considered the most vulnerable part of the bill. The Supreme Court held that there were ample precedents in prior decisions and examples of corruption in political conduct to abolish soft money and to place restrictions on sham issue ads. Moreover, as the bill's backers carefully drafted it and guided it through Congress, they had two criteria: that Congress would approve it and that it would be held constitutional. In doing so, they made compromises, but they nevertheless enacted a significant reform bill.

In taking the steps they did, Congress, and then the Supreme Court, put an end to, or at least severely limited, the "shakedown": the implicit, and sometimes explicit, understanding that there will be favors in exchange for a contributor's money, whether access to a candidate, a call to a regulatory agency, or consideration of a contributor's interests when it comes time for congressional votes. They can affect regulations by the numerous federal agencies. Contributions may influence whether a bill will be considered and what it will contain.

The concern for raising money indisputably affects the votes of elected officeholders. Dick Durbin, the Democratic senator from Illinois, candidly told me a few years ago that when he went to the floor, he couldn't avoid thinking about how his vote might affect future contributions. In Washington, access, or the illusion of it, is practically everything. It's the beginning point for achieving one's purposes. The shakedowns could take the form of a conversation or something more elaborate and head-spinning: the $50,000 "coffees" and sleepovers during the Clinton administration; cruises; golfing weekends.

On the face of it, one would be tempted to conclude that the Bush administration, sympathetic as it is to corporate interests, is no less corrupt than Clinton's in skewing policy in the anticipation of, or as a reward for, contributions; but Trevor Potter, a former chairman of the Federal Election Committee and now head of the pro-reform Campaign Legal Center, argues that the Bush administration's policies in favor of business arise from genuine beliefs, not corruption. He points out that the highest officials, Bush and Cheney, come from the corporate world and have been formed by it. The Bush administration's actions in cutting taxes, gutting regulations, and doing large favors for the energy, coal, steel, and drug industries, Potter argues, have been propelled by a pro-business ideology, and, in the case of the coal and steel industries, also by the desire to win votes in crucial industrial states (Ohio, Pennsylvania, Michigan, and West Virginia). That's not corruption; it's American democracy as we know it. The result is that the rich and powerful have more access and influence than ordinary citizens. That certain industries raise a great deal of money for Bush, Potter says, is a result of the policies that the administration follows, not the impetus for them. "When they want to do energy policy they summon the energy companies because that's who they know and where they're coming from," Potter told me recently.

Yet now, with individual donations strictly limited, candidates for office may still feel beholden to people who gather a large number of $2,000 or lesser contributions from employees, friends, and the names in their rolodexes. The 2000 Bush campaign had its "Pioneers," who raised $100,000. Now Bush has added a new category, Rangers, who raise $200,000. Such "bundling" is not illegal, but reformers' efforts to abolish it have been blocked, mainly by congresswomen who are protecting EMILY'S List, which backs pro-choice Democratic women running for office. So large fund-raisers are still courted, flattered, and appointed, and reformers will continue to press for outlawing "bundling."

Already various groups have been formed by close allies of both political parties, to act as conduits for large contributions to candidates for the 2004 election. (Democrats have set up the Media Fund, run by longtime Clinton loyalist Harold Ickes, and America Coming Together; Republicans have established Americans for a Better Country and the Leadership Forum.) Reformers have filed a court case arguing that such dummy committees are illegal. (The Republicans' outrage over contributions of more than ten million dollars by the financier George Soros to groups backing Democrats is a splendid example of political hypocrisy.[5])

McCain and the other sponsors of the new campaign finance law foresaw that there would be efforts to get around it, but they consider finance reform a continuing process in which reformers try to fix the most blatant problems; and then, when a new problem arises and a consensus can be formed that something must be done, they move on to the new one. Though the reformers can take satisfaction from what they have achieved so far, they know that they already have new problems to deal with.

Unlike 2000, this time the voters know that it matters a great deal who is elected president. Almost everything the federal government does, therefore every citizen, is affected. The President has formidable advantages: the constant publicity that comes with occupying the White House; vast amounts of money; the power to affect at least some events; the ability to perform what may be convincing stunts. He may have lucky breaks, such as the capture of bin Laden, before the election.

Bush's denigrators to the contrary, he isn't dumb. He is inarticulate, uncurious, and anti-intellectual, to be sure, but also shrewd in limited but important ways: in meetings he is said to go quickly to the main point,[6] and he's a very effective politician. According to polls, much of the public finds him genial and easygoing, which is a political advantage, even if it's a deceptive impression. Like his mother, who also puts on a good show, Bush is tough on those around him and he can be mean. One often hears the fuzzy proposition that many Americans want to like their president and that, with some exceptions, they usually vote for the seemingly more likable candidate.

Still, Bush is not at this stage unbeatable: his foreign and economic policies have stirred widespread opposition.

According to John Zogby's polling, even after the capture of Saddam Hussein only 45–47 percent of respondents said they would vote to reelect him—not at all a good sign for a supposedly popular president. A great deal will depend on unpredictable events.

—January 14, 2004

FOOTNOTES

1 See my article on Rove, "The Enforcer," pp. 1–19.

2 Santorum stated in April 2003 that if the Supreme Court says you have the right to gay sex "within your home, then you have the right to bigamy, you have the right to polygamy, you have the right to incest, you have the right to adultery. You have the right to anything."

3 For a view of a different Senate at a different time, see Don Oberdorfer, *Senator Mansfield: The Extraordinary Life of a Great American Statesman and Diplomat* (Smithsonian Books, 2003).

4 For a fascinating history of how the House has developed, see Nelson W. Polsby, *How Congress Evolves: Social Bases of Institutional Change* (Oxford University Press, 2003).

5 For Soros's angry indictment of the Bush administration's foreign and antiterrorist policies, see his recent book, *The Bubble of American Supremacy: Correcting the Misuse of American Power* (PublicAffairs, 2003).

6 For a contrasting view, see the comments of Paul O'Neill, former secretary of the treasury, in Ron Suskind's book *The Price of Loyalty* (Simon and Schuster, 2004).

LABYRINTH BOOKS

536 West 112th Street
NY NY 10025
Ph.212-865-1588 Fax 212-865-2749
www.labyrinthbooks.com
email: books@labyrinthbooks.com

77788 Reg 6 8:03 am 09/13/04

Sales for Customer #100578

S FEAR & LOATHING I	1 @	7.95	7.95
SUBTOTAL			7.95
SALES TAX - 8.625%			.69
TOTAL			8.64
MASTER CARD PAYMENT			8.64

Account# XXXXXXXXXXXX3039 Exp Date 0906
Authorization# 013436

I agree to pay the above total amount
according to the card issuer agreement.

Purchased 97.53 towards 100.00

ORDER FROM ANYWHERE, WE SHIP EVERYWHERE
Hours m-f 9am-10pm sa 10-8 su 11-7
RETURNS ACCEPTED ONLY WITHIN 10 DAYS
AND WITH A RECEIPT.
NO REFUNDS, STORE CREDIT ONLY.

7788 Reg E   8:03 am 03/13/04

Sales for Customer #100578

MASTER CARD PAYMENT		8.64

I agree to pay the above total amount
according to the card issuer agreement.

Purchased 97.52 towards 100.00

The New York Review of Books

The New York Review of Books, published twenty times each year, has been called "the country's most successful intellectual journal." (*The New York Times*)

To find out more, including how to subscribe, visit our website: www.nybooks.com. Or call or write:

The New York Review of Books
1755 Broadway
New York, New York 10019
Telephone: (212) 757-8070
Fax: (212) 333-5374
Email: nyrsub@nybooks.com